Festivals *of the* World

TRINIDAD

Gareth Stevens Publishing
MILWAUKEE

Written by
ROYSTON ELLIS

Edited by
FIONA CONBOY

Designed by
HASNAH MOHD ESA

Picture research by
SUSAN JANE MANUEL

First published in North America in 1999 by
Gareth Stevens Publishing
1555 North RiverCenter Drive, Suite 201
Milwaukee, Wisconsin 53212 USA

For a free color catalog describing Gareth
Stevens' list of high-quality books and multimedia
programs, call
1-800-542-2595 (USA)
or 1-800-461-9120 (Canada).
Gareth Stevens Publishing's Fax: (414) 225-0377.

© **TIMES EDITIONS PTE LTD 1999**
Originated and designed by
Times Books International
an imprint of Times Editions Pte Ltd
Times Centre, 1 New Industrial Road
Singapore 536196
Printed in Malaysia

Library of Congress Cataloging-in-Publication Data:
Ellis, Royston, 1941–
Trinidad / by Royston Ellis.
p. cm. — (Festivals of the world)
Includes bibliographical references and index.
Summary: Describes how the culture of Trinidad is
reflected in its many festivals, including Carnival,
Phagwa, Hosay, and Parang.
ISBN 0-8368-2036-3 (lib. bdg.)
1. Festivals—Trinidad—Juvenile literature.
2. Trinidad—Social life and customs—
Juvenile literature. [1. Festivals—Trinidad.
2. Holidays—Trinidad. 3. Trinidad—Social life
and customs.] I. Title. II. Series
GT4829.T7E45 1999
394.2697283—dc21 99-18310

1 2 3 4 5 6 7 8 9 03 02 01 00 99

CONTENTS

It's Festival Time . . .

Life in Trinidad is like a year-long *fete* [FET]—that's how Trinidadians describe a party. Trinidad is a tropical country where people love to have fun. There is probably a steel band concert, a calypso show, a *chutney* [CHUT-nee] performance, a parade, a village festival, or a street party going on somewhere in Trinidad every day of the year. This joyful island in the sun has many forms of music and dance. So come for a visit and enjoy the fete!

WHERE'S TRINIDAD?

Trinidad is a beautiful island in the Caribbean that lies north of the South American country of Venezuela. About 50 miles (80 kilometers) long and 40 miles (64 km) wide, it is the larger island of the nation known as Trinidad and Tobago.

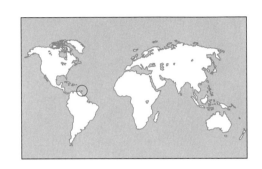

Who are the Trinidadians?

There are just over 1.2 million people living in Trinidad. They are called Trinidadians, or Trinis. They are an interesting blend of people from South America, Africa, Spain, France, Britain, and Portugal, who first settled in Trinidad about 400 years ago. The Africans were brought to the country as slaves, but when slavery became illegal, workers came from India. Today, about 40 percent of the population are of African descent and another 40 percent are of East Indian descent. Most of the remainder are of mixed **heritage**.

After many years of British rule, Trinidad became an independent country in 1962. The official language is English. More than 60 percent of the population are Christian, a quarter are Hindu, and 6 percent are Muslim. The others follow traditional African faiths.

Trinidadians of all ages have lots of fun. They love to play music, sing, and dance.

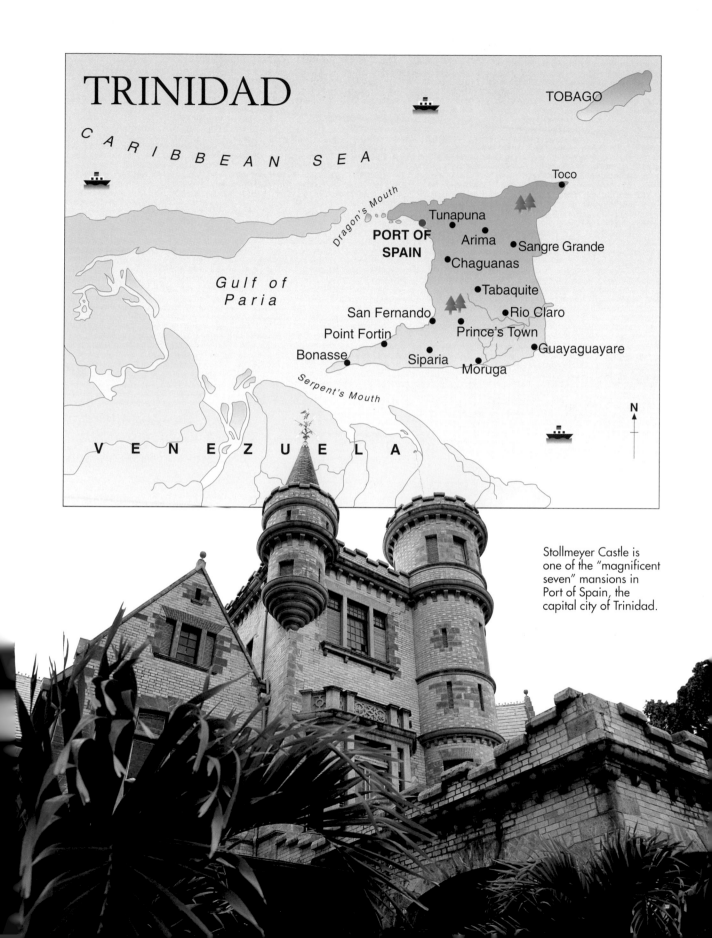

TRINIDAD

TOBAGO

C A R I B B E A N   S E A

Dragon's Mouth

Toco

Tunapuna

PORT OF SPAIN

Arima

Sangre Grande

Chaguanas

Gulf of Paria

Tabaquite

San Fernando

Rio Claro

Point Fortin

Prince's Town

Bonasse

Guayaguayare

Siparia

Moruga

Serpent's Mouth

V E N E Z U E L A

N

Stollmeyer Castle is one of the "magnificent seven" mansions in Port of Spain, the capital city of Trinidad.

WHEN'S THE FETE?

I have my costume on, and I'm ready for the Carnival parade! Come to the kids' Carnival on page 11.

SEASONAL FESTIVALS

✪ **CARNIVAL** —Trinidad is world famous for its Carnival, held each year on the Monday and Tuesday before Ash Wednesday. People parade through the streets wearing spectacular costumes, singing songs, and dancing to steel band music.

✪ **EASTER** — Highlights of the Easter holidays are goat and crab races, held on Trinidad's sister island of Tobago.

✪ **PARANG**

✪ **CHRISTMAS** — Christmas floats, performing troupes, mascots, marching bands, and Santa Claus parade the streets of Port of Spain starting in November. Shops, sidewalks, and streets are adorned with brilliant Christmas decorations. Steel bands add a tropical flavor to Christmas celebrations in Trinidad.

MUSLIM FESTIVALS

✪ **EID EL-FITR**—Worship in mosques and ritual feasting mark the end of Ramadan.

✪ **HOSAY**—The annual Hosay Festival is Islamic in origin. This three-day spectacular of color and rhythm starts on a different date each year. Drummers and dancers carry symbolic crescent moons to the sea and set them adrift.

HINDU FESTIVALS

✪ **DIVALI**—This Hindu Festival of Light is both a religious event and a display of Hindu culture.

✪ **PHAGWA**—This colorful festival at the time of the Hindu New Year features some unusual traditions.

✪ **RAMLEELA**—Communities join together and act out stories from Hindu scriptures, while dancers perform, at the longest running—held over nine days—street fair in the Caribbean.

The music of steel drum bands is a familiar sound on the island of Trinidad.

NATIONAL FESTIVALS

✪ **EMANCIPATION DAY**—A seven-day festival commemorates the end of slavery in Trinidad in 1838.

✪ **INDIAN ARRIVAL DAY**—This public holiday recalls the arrival, in 1845, of the first settlers from India, who came to work on Trinidad's plantations.

✪ **STEEL BAND WEEK**—Steel bands echo through the streets of Port of Spain in this week-long festival celebrating music unique to Trinidad.

✪ **INDEPENDENCE DAY**—This celebration includes a parade of military bands and fireworks displayed in a huge park.

CARNIVAL

Trinidadians describe their Carnival as "the biggest party on Earth." Anyone who has seen or taken part in this special Caribbean festival would agree with them.

All night party!

Carnival came to Trinidad with the French Roman Catholic plantation owners in the 18th century. While the rich held **masquerade** balls on the night before **Lent**, their slaves celebrated around the cooking fires with songs and dances. Today, Carnival is enjoyed by every Trinidadian and visitor, whatever his or her religion or economic status. The first Carnival parade begins at dawn on the Monday before Ash Wednesday, and the partying goes on day and night. Carnival doesn't end until midnight the following day!

A magnificent display of color

Carnival features parades of bands with nonstop music and amazing costumes, a Carnival King and Queen, and an atmosphere of fun that makes everyone feel good.

It takes hours for every costume band to reach the main stage at a huge park in Port of Spain. Crowds jam the grandstands to watch the revelers dance across the stage displaying their magnificent costumes. People line the streets and cheer as their favorite bands pass by.

Left: The best band and the best costumes all win prizes at Carnival.

Opposite: Every year, Trinis compete with each other to make their Carnival display the most spectacular parade in the world.

Getting ready for Carnival

In the weeks leading up to Carnival, the members of each costume band meet at mas [MAAS] camp, where the costumes are made. *Mas* is short for "masquerade."

Each group of revelers has its own band. It might be a calypso band with brass and guitars or a steel band with drums called pans. Some steel bands have up to 100 musicians playing 400 instruments made out of oil drums.

For weeks before Carnival, calypso singers perform for the crowds that come to their shows. Calypso songs are written for each Carnival and have funny lyrics about **topical** themes. The most popular song becomes the Carnival "Road March." Thousands of people sing it as the colorful procession winds through the streets of Port of Spain.

Each band wears costumes depicting a particular theme.

Carnival costumes are often made of fabric stretched over frames. Some are so heavy they have to be wheeled along.

Kids' Carnival

Children in Trinidad are very lucky. They have their own Carnival, held on the Saturday before the main event. Thousands of children, from tiny tots to teenagers, put on costumes made by their parents and friends and parade through the town. Each child belongs to a well-organized group, led by its own steel band and amplified calypso music. The children have a wonderful time, whether they are taking part or just watching.

Hours of work went into creating this elaborate costume. It is bigger than the little girl wearing it!

Think about this

Children love to have fun, and fun often seems better and easier to have when you're doing something with friends. In Trinidad, young and old alike become members of special groups, so they can take part in Carnival together. Do you know any groups that do things together? It might be fun to join them!

PHAGWA

Imagine a festival devoted to squirting people with colored water! Wouldn't it be fun? Well, that is just what happens at the Phagwa [fag-WAH] festival in Trinidad. Phagwa is celebrated by Trinidadians with Indian roots. Held near the end of March, it marks the season of the Hindu New Year. Of course, all Trinis love a party, so many who are not Hindu join in the festival, too! Not only is it lots of fun, but it is also a dramatic way to end spring and start summer.

Religious plays

Preparations for Phagwa begin months in advance. Activities during this fete include nightly *chowtal* [CHOW-tahl] singing competitions, in which the best singers win prizes for their skills. Plays are performed in the villages, too, and, since the Hindu religion is the basis of Phagwa, religious stories, such as the legend of Holika, are acted out.

According to Hindu **lore**, Holika was the evil sister of King Kiranya Kashipu. To punish his son, Prahlada, for not worshiping him as a god, the King sent Holika to carry Prahlada into a bonfire. God protected Prahlada, and the young boy escaped unhurt, but his evil aunt burned to death. Bonfires are lit at night during Phagwa as symbols of Holika's destruction.

Hindu singing and dancing are accompanied by special instruments. One instrument, called a *dholak* [DOH-lack], is a small drum made with goat skin. Cymbals, called *kartals* [car-TAHLS], are also used to liven up the music.

Dancing the night away

Trinidad's own music, called chutney, has become popular throughout the island and can be heard during Phagwa. Chutney is a popular East Indian dance music with a fast-paced, highly danceable beat. It originated in Trinidad but has its roots in the folk songs sung at Hindu weddings and birth ceremonies.

Dancing, whether in village streets or at chutney performances, is an important part of Phagwa. The style unique to Trinidad is a combination of the graceful, mystic movements of folkloric East Indian dances and the lively waist-twisting gyrations of Afro-Caribbean heritage. Traditional Hindu dancing is also performed at Phagwa.

Hindu dancers at the Phagwa celebrations are both graceful and colorful.

Stories on the move

In recent years, parades of floats have been added to Phagwa celebrations. The floats are built on trucks and represent scenes and events from Hindu stories. Beauty contests are held to select pretty girls to grace the floats. The girls wear exotic costumes with an Indian theme and stand on the floats as the parade passes through towns and villages. Bands playing calypso and chutney lead the way, so the beauty queens have music wherever they go.

Think about this
Throwing colored water at someone is not a nice thing to do, but, in Trinidad, people don't always mind. At the Phagwa festival, they know they are going to get messy. Do you celebrate any festivals by getting other people dirty?

Opposite: Soaked with colored water and smeared with powder paints, Phagwa festivalgoers gather to watch singing competitions and lighthearted plays.

The Festival of Colors

The highlight of Phagwa is the Festival of Colors. It is supposed to celebrate both the life of a legendary holy boy called Prahlada, which means Joy, and the immortal love of Lord Krishna for a beautiful girl named Radha. On this day, everybody squirts colored water at each other and smears each other with scarlet powder. The water is called *abeer* [ab-EER]. It is a bright liquid made with vegetable dye, and it gets everywhere, drenching clothes and covering spectators with a messy purple coating.

People know what is going to happen at the Festival of Colors, and many participants wear white clothes just for the fun of seeing them change color! This **spontaneous** painting of people is an art form known as *pichakaree* (pee-CHAH-kah-ree).

HOSAY

I n Trinidad, each religion has its own festival. Christians have Carnival, Hindus have Phagwa, and Muslims have Hosay [hoh-SAY]. Although at one time it was a solemn affair, Hosay is a celebration in Trinidad today.

A time to remember

Hosay was not always the joyful occasion it is today. When it was first celebrated in 1884, it commemorated the famous **massacre** of brothers Hussein and Hassan, grandsons of the prophet Mohammed, during the Holy War in Persia in A.D. 680. In countries such as Iran (formerly Persia), Iraq, Lebanon, and India, some Muslims see this festival as a time of deep mourning.

The Muslims who came to Trinidad from India tried to remember the occasion with a proper ceremony. As years passed and the original settlers died, the form of Hosay changed to include all the color and excitement of a Muslim version of Carnival. The African habit of turning funeral **rites** into joyful occasions also influenced Hosay, and, today, many non-Muslims take part in the celebrations, too.

Each Hosay festival follows a set pattern, with *tadjahs* [TAH-djars], models representing the tombs of the brothers, featured in processions.

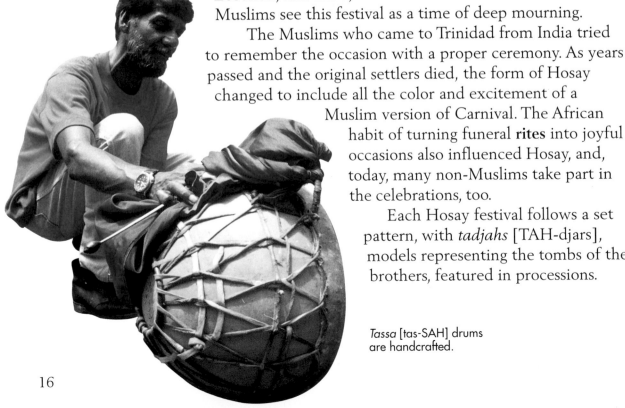

The flags displayed on Flag Night are symbols of the famous battle in which Hussein and Hassan were killed.

Tassa [tas-SAH] drums are handcrafted.

16

Parades and processions

Hosay stretches over three nights, beginning with Flag Night, when hundreds of people parade through the streets carrying flags. After the parade, the flags are displayed on a platform where incense is being burned, filling the air with the sweet fragrance of sandalwood.

In a procession on the second night, dancers carry small tadjahs on their heads. At midnight, the dancers gently touch the tadjahs against each other to symbolize uniting the two brothers.

On the third night, large tadjahs, as much as 9 feet (2.7 meters) tall, are wheeled through the streets, accompanied by dancers and drummers. Throughout the evening, the throb of tassa drums fills the air. The tassa is a large wooden drum slung across the chest of the drummer, who slaps the tassa with his hands to produce its deep, throbbing sound.

Tassa drummers lead the procession of beautifully crafted model tombs.

17

Dancing moons

Two of the dancers accompanying the large tadjahs carry curve-shaped structures that are 6 feet (1.8 m) long and 3 feet (1 m) high. These structures are crescent moons, and they represent the brothers. One is usually red, in honor of Hussein, who was beheaded. The other, which is green or blue, honors Hassan. A traditional Indian dance, performed with expressive movements of arms and legs, represents the brothers' triumph over death. At midnight, the dancers carrying the moons slowly approach each other in a ritual that symbolizes brotherly embrace. At that wonderful moment, the spectators cheer.

The Hosay festival comes to an end the following morning. The tadjahs and the moons are brought out for the last time and are carried in a procession of prayers and offerings to the sea. There, from Trinidad's shores, they are set adrift, carrying the spirit of Hosay with them until next year's festival.

Below: The crescent moons are decorated with hundreds of pieces of brightly colored tissue paper. After the procession, they are laid down in honor of the brothers, before they are taken to the sea.

Think about this

Have you ever seen a crescent moon? The moon is lit by the sun and goes through a cycle of phases, one of which makes it look like a crescent, or a canoe, floating in the sky. Do you know what the different phases of the moon are?

Opposite: The model tombs are heavy and require a team of people to wheel them along in the procession.

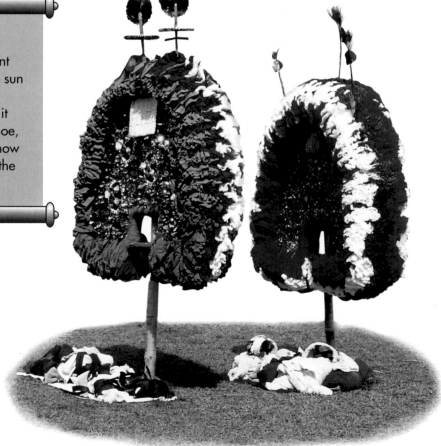

DIVALI

The Hindu Festival of Light is called Divali [dee-VAL-ee]. It is a time when twinkling flames, like little stars, light up the hillsides of Trinidad, glow in gardens and parks, and shine throughout the night in towns and villages.

Right: Divali lights symbolize the power of good over evil, light over darkness, and intelligence over ignorance.

A row of lights

Divali is a shortened form of the word *Deepavali*, which means "row of lights." The main night of the festival falls every year in the month of Kartik in the Hindu calendar, which is usually in late October or early November.

Preparations begin a few weeks before Divali, when bamboo poles are cut and used to build platforms for small clay pots, called *dayas* [dye-AS]. The pots are filled with coconut oil, and a short **wick** is placed in each one.

As darkness falls on the evening of Divali, the dayas are lit, and the houses, streets, and hills of Trinidad glitter with tiny, flickering lights. The dayas are tended carefully so they stay lit throughout the night.

Divali is a special time of peace and goodwill for the Hindus of Trinidad.

Peace and goodwill

Lighting the dayas is done in honor of the Hindu goddess of light, Lakshmi, who is also considered the goddess of beauty, riches, and love. Lakshmi is very important to Hindus, and everybody wants to treat her well. During Divali, people make special offerings and pray to Lakshmi at ceremonies called *pujas* [poo-JAHS]. They also worship the goddess with songs and the chanting of **mantras**. In statues and paintings, Lakshmi is portrayed holding a lotus blossom. To many Hindus in Trinidad, the lotus represents fertility, spiritual power, and purity. Because Lakshmi's fame through the Festival of Light has fascinated many Trinidadians who are not Hindus, they, too, join in the celebrations. Compared with celebrations for other festivals, Divali is a quiet festival. It is a day of peace and goodwill.

This temple shrine honors Lakshmi, the goddess of light.

21

Gifts of food

Traditional Hindus begin the main day of Divali by getting up before sunrise and bathing in oil. They say prayers, put on new clothes, and go to the temple to worship. Afterward, they visit the elders in the family to offer their respect.

In each Hindu home, special sweets prepared for Divali are set out for guests. People exchange greetings, and gifts of food are presented to neighbors, the poor, and to non-Hindu friends who visit on the main day of the festival.

All guests share in a food, called *parsad* [pah-SAD], made especially as an offering to the gods. Parsad is very sweet. It is made with flour, sugar, milk, and raisins.

Above: Lots of delicious sweet treats are served in Trinidadian homes at Divali celebrations.

People from each village share dayas for decorating their streets and buildings.

Above: Pottery factory workers are busy making dayas for weeks before Divali.

The Divali queen

Popular with almost every Trinidadian are the shows and pageants that lead up to the night of lights. In recent years, these shows have become very exciting, with famous Indian musicians taking part. Song competitions, featuring the works of local composers, are held before large audiences. Oriental dancing and traditional songs are also performed. There are many competitions to select a local Divali queen, who takes part in the pageantry of this peaceful feast. Divali is an interesting combination of religious observance, local Hindu culture, and the triumph of light over darkness.

The Divali queen wears traditional Hindu garments during the Festival of Light.

23

PARANG

Christmas starts early in Trinidad. Its coming is heralded by Parang [pa-RANG]. This festival begins in November and goes on until January. It is a time when roving bands of musicians drop in on neighbors, without warning, to bring them the unique and exciting sound of Parang music.

Sounds of Spain

Parang music began as Spanish-inspired Christmas songs. These songs were first performed in Trinidad when it was a Spanish colony. The colony ended in 1797, but the Parang tradition has survived over 200 years. It has endured because of Trinidad's contacts with Spanish-speaking Venezuela, which is only 10 miles (16 km) away on the South American mainland. With French, African, and English words added to the Spanish lyrics, the result is a joyful tribute to Christmas that delights young and old alike, even if the meaning of the songs is difficult to understand.

Parang music shows its South American roots with its lively beat. Trinidadians and tourists love to dance to the Parang rhythm.

All night music

When Parang musicians start playing their instruments and singing outside a home, its doors are opened eagerly. The musicians settle down to play and sing throughout the night. Everyone in the house, including the children, forgets about sleep and joins in the singing. The music goes on until dawn.

The main instrument in a Parang band is the *cuatro* [koo-AH-troh], a tiny four-stringed guitar. Acoustic guitars and mandolins are also played, accompanied by violins and **maracas**.

For Trinidadians, Parang conjures up Christmas magic the same way singing carols does in many other countries.

Above: Parang tunes bring the spirit of Christmas to Trinidad.

The musicians who play in Parang bands are known as *paranderos* [pa-ran-DAIR-roes].

25

Things For You To Do

Trinidad is famous for its steel band music, its calypso songs, and the amazing costumes created for Carnival. If you visited Trinidad during Carnival, you would certainly see some spectacular costumes and hear some beautiful music.

Dress up for Carnival

Some Carnival partyers spend weeks making their elaborate headdresses and outfits. On the night before Carnival, many people disguise themselves as devils, beggars, or old women. You and your friends could make headdresses, costumes, and disguises at your very own mas camp.

To make a Carnival headdress, you will need colored cardboard, tissue paper, and marker pens. You can make the headdress as simple or complicated as you want. As long as the colors are bright, it will always fit in at Carnival!

Create your own steel band

Steel band music is a sound for which Trinidadians are famous. The drums, called pans, are traditionally made out of a metal barrel, or drum. One of the flat ends is curved inward and portions of it are raised. Each portion of the drum makes a different sound when it is struck with a rubber-tipped stick, or mallet.

Steel drummers use their skill to create a gentle, magical sound. It takes a long time to master the art of playing steel drums, but you and your friends could collect some tins and bottles to make an old-fashioned steel band. In the early days, Trinis used old cans to create the rhythm that is now made on steel drums. See if you can create some Trini music of your own!

Things to look for in your library

Calypso Callaloo... Donald Hill (University Press of Florida, 1993).
Carnival, Camboulay and Calypso: Traditions in the Making. John Cowley (Cambridge University Press, 1996).
History of the People of Trinidad and Tobago. Eric Williams (A & B Book Publishers, 1993).
Jump Up Time: A Trinidad Carnival Story. Lynn Joseph (Clarion Books, 1998).
A Little Salmon for Witness: A Story from Trinidad. Vashanti Rahaman (Lodestar Books, 1997).
Teach Yourself to Play Pan. Sherman Fyfe (Major & Minor Productions, 1996).
Trinidad and Tobago. Patricia Vrosevich (Chelsea House Publishing, 1998).
Trinidad and Tobago. (http://city.net/countries/trinidad_and_tobago/, 1999).

MAKE A PAPER MOON

T rinidadians are great costume designers. To them, a costume is an artistic creation with lots of color, sequins, ribbons, and other trimmings.

In Trinidad's Hosay Festival, two dancers carry elaborate paper moons. These moons are bigger than a child, at least 6 feet (1.8 m) long by 3 feet (1 m) wide, and they are not round. They are crescent-shaped moons. Why don't you try making your own paper crescent moon?

You will need:
1. Round stick or dowel 18" (45 cm)
2. Cardboard, 11.5" x 16.5" (29 cm x 42 cm)
3. Colored paper
4. Tape
5. Glue
6. Scissors
7. Pencil
8. Gold foil

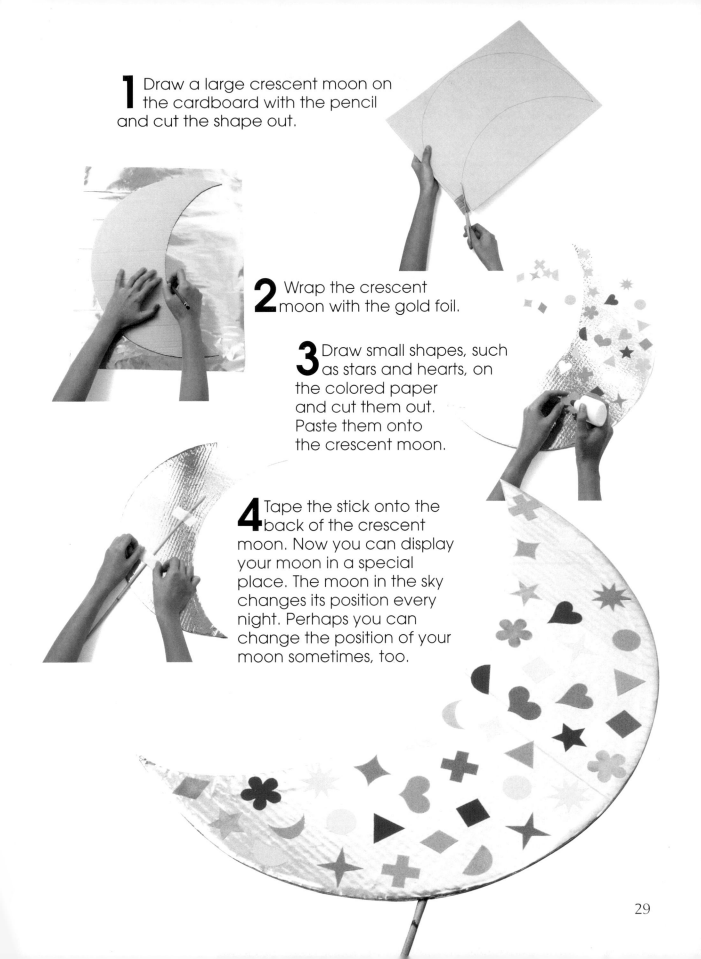

1 Draw a large crescent moon on the cardboard with the pencil and cut the shape out.

2 Wrap the crescent moon with the gold foil.

3 Draw small shapes, such as stars and hearts, on the colored paper and cut them out. Paste them onto the crescent moon.

4 Tape the stick onto the back of the crescent moon. Now you can display your moon in a special place. The moon in the sky changes its position every night. Perhaps you can change the position of your moon sometimes, too.

MAKE CALLALOO

Callaloo is a savory green soup that is very popular in Trinidad. The word *callaloo* is also used to describe any mix of races, cultures, or personalities. Callaloo is, therefore, a soup made from a mix of different kinds of green vegetables. In Trinidad, one of the leaves used is from the **dasheen** plant, which is a kind of yam. You can use spinach, instead.

You will need:

1. 2 pounds (1 kg) spinach leaves
2. 12 sliced okra pods
3. 1 diced green bell pepper
4. 3 crushed cloves of garlic
5. 2 chopped chives
6. 1 chopped onion
7. 1 chicken bouillon cube
8. 1 teaspoon salt
9. 1 teaspoon pepper
10. ½ teaspoon thyme
11. 2½ cups (600 ml) of water
12. Large saucepan
13. Cutting board
14. Measuring spoons
15. Ladle
16. Measuring cup

12

11 and 16

4 and 5

1 and 13

6

7, 8, 9, and 10

15

14

2

3

1 Wash the spinach leaves and tear them into shreds.

2 Put the water into the saucepan with all the other ingredients. Ask an adult to put the saucepan on the stove over low heat.

3 After the soup starts to boil, let it simmer 30 minutes, stirring occasionally. When it begins to thicken, it is ready to eat. Add salt and pepper to taste. Ladle the callaloo into two bowls and serve it with bread and butter.

GLOSSARY

INDEX

Picture credits
A. N. A. Press Agency: 26 (top); Stephen Broadridge: 16 (top); DDB Stock Photo: 10 (bottom), 26 (bottom); Tor Eigeland: 7 (bottom), 8, 9, 11, 15; HBL: 25 (top); Dave G. Houser: 5; The Hutchison Library: 6; Images Studio: 3 (bottom), 4, 12, 13, 14, 16 (bottom), 17, 18, 19, 20 (top), 22 (top), 23 (both), 24, 25 (bottom), 27, 28; David Simson: 1, 2, 3 (top), 7 (top), 20 (bottom), 21 (both); Vision Photo Agency: 10 (top); Norbert Wu/Mo Yung Productions: 22 (bottom)

Digital scanning by
Superskill Graphics Pte Ltd.